IMAGES
of Sport

MERTHYR TYDFIL
FOOTBALL CLUB

A cartoon from the Atalanta programme *Nerazzurro*. The editorial in this publication read as follows:

'Our newspaper is delighted to extend a very warm welcome to our friends from Wales on behalf of all Bergamo sports lovers. Whatever the result of the match may be, regardless of who qualifies for the next round, we shall certainly never forget you. It is a rare quality, and one we greatly admire, to approach a match as you do, and certainly this quality is not seen in Italy today. You see matches as an opportunity to enjoy a sporting event, to meet friends, to applaud your opponents if they deserve it. These things are no longer seen here. So, a special thank you to the friends of Merthyr Tydfil for the welcome you gave us a couple of weeks ago, for the Italian flags, and for the party held in Atalanta's honour. We don't know if we can rise to the occasion quite so well, but one thing's certain – you deserve festivities in your honour ten times greater than these. Regardless of the outcome and who goes on into the next round, it has been a great pleasure for us to meet you'.

IMAGES
of Sport

MERTHYR TYDFIL
FOOTBALL CLUB

Compiled by
David Watkins

TEMPUS

First published 1999
Copyright © David Watkins, 1999

Tempus Publishing Limited
The Mill, Brimscombe Port,
Stroud, Gloucestershire, GL5 2QG

ISBN 0 7524 1813 0

Typesetting and origination by
Tempus Publishing Limited
Printed in Great Britain by
Midway Clark Printing, Wiltshire

Penydarren Park, home of Merthyr Tydfil Football Club.

Contents

Foreword

Our Martyrs will be playing in the Football League in the New Millennium! Roll On!

That is the dream of fans and well-wishers, plus the strong belief of soccer's Three Wise Men – John Charles, Trevor Ford and Tommy Docherty. Player-manager King John treasures his years at Merthyr as the happiest of his superstar career. With a heavyweight chuckle, he recalls, 'I played, drove the team bus and called bingo numbers for chairman Maldwyn Davies at the Theatre Royal!'

Merthyr gets you in the nicest way. My old mate Trevor Ford keeps telling me the whole town is now talking soccer again. In his own words, 'Yes, the Martyrs will be back big-time. The real crime was that they kicked cash-struggling Merthyr Town out of the old Third Division in the depression of the 1930s because they owed a lousy £516 – big deal! That would be very small change these days to millionaires David Beckham and Alan Shearer. I wish Merthyr could repay it and sue for the years money can't buy back'.

I've been several times recently to Penydarren Park (where Ford was Aston Villa's striker as they lost 7-4 in the make-right match for Syd Howarth's £6,500 transfer). The place is buzzing again with the Just Players set up.

'Yes I agree with Charlo, look out for Merthyr this new season and certainly in the New Millennium. My money is on them to do very, very well, and much sooner than people think' – Tommy Docherty, still top of the After-Dinner Speakers League, and a regular visitor to Wales, emphasises, 'Soccer will go through the roof after Year 2000. But we must keep a place for Merthyr in the new streamlined league structures'.

Merthyr's specific future? The Doc prescribed 'Finding another Bill Hullett would give them a £10 million start, on today's prices. I've got my losing memories of trying to outjump him in my Preston days. We called him Birdman Bill! He went up, stayed there – and then the ball was in our net. Hullett's conveyor belt of goals continued with ace goalscorers David Webley, Gordon Davies, Ray Pratt, Nick Deacey – all after Jenkin Powell, Bill Jarman, Stan Davies and tearaway Trevor Reynolds, each following in the footsteps of the Welsh sporting Messiah.

Now, its look-ahead time for the Martyrs, especially in the challenge of the New Millennium. Cheers and roll on 2,000 plus!

John Lloyd
an original *Merthyr Express* candac and *Daily Express* sportswriter

Introduction

The pride which a football club brings to its town and surrounding area is beyond price. A touch of fame, fleeting fortune and, yes, times of failure amounting even to despair, are all compounded in the emotions of a club's supporters. Those strange sensations are whipped together in an alchemy that passes on from one generation to the next.

It all began for Merthyr in 1908. A group of zealous sportsmen introduced Merthyr Town FC to the original Southern League. Apart from the first season and the 1914-18 war years they played at this level until 1920. From then to 1930 they graced the Football League itself.

Soccer brought cherished relief from the cruel economic depression that battered the town. However, the club could not escape the financial whirlwind that was blowing everywhere. First it was back to non-League, and in 1934 the club was disbanded. Eleven fallow soccer years passed by. Then, in 1945, new enthusiasts captured the spirit of the post-war age by setting up Merthyr Tydfil AFC. After borrowing kit and footballs to hold trial matches they joined the Welsh League and, in the following season, the Southern League.

In an astonishing opening nine years of their new life Merthyr won The Welsh FA Cup twice, The Southern League five times, the Southern League Cup twice, the Welsh League twice, and the South Wales and Monmouthshire Cup three times. In seven of these seasons Merthyr scored more than 100 Southern League goals. Their lowest tally was a mere 84. Thousands of supporters flowed into Penydarren Park week by week in a fever of anticipation. It was the nearest wonder people had experienced to the religious revival that fired hearts and minds throughout the Valleys. Years of ups and, often tremulous, downs followed. They have included a passage in the Football Conference and glory in Europe with victory over Atalanta of Italy in 1987.

This book gives a fascinating insight into the whole of the period. For his painstaking work in compiling it, David Watkins deserves our gratitude. We should not forget to be grateful, too, to the host of men and women who have led and supported Merthyr football throughout this century.

John Rees
an original *Merthyr Express* candac and former editor of the *Western Mail*.

Merthyr striker David Webley takes on the Atalanta defence. David Webley was an extraordinary goal-getter, scoring from all angles and against any opposition. He had the knack of being on the right spot at the right time. David was regularly among the goals during Merthyr's rise to the Vauxhall Conference, turning in superb displays that attracted the attention of many League clubs.

One
Merthyr Town FC
1908-20

Merthyr A.F.C. 1908-9.

The original Merthyr Town FC was formed in 1908 and the club was one of the pioneers of professional football in South Wales, being elected to the Southern League Second Division in 1909. The club's debut at Penydarren Park was on Saturday 5 September 1908 when Swansea Town (as they were then) provided the opposition in a friendly that ended in a 2-1 defeat.

The history of Penydarren Park goes back to the Roman invasion of Wales in AD 74-78. Two legions were despatched to the area, many of the legionaries being based at Penydarren Park. The fort at the site was probably erected during this period, but traces of it were not discovered until 1786. Evacuations commenced properly in 1902 when the site was proposed as the town's football pitch.

Penydarren Place (or as it was also called Penydarren House) was the first luxurious house in Merthyr. This splendid mansion house was built by Samuel Homfray, one of Merthyr Tydfil's early ironmasters, in 1786. The building was situated at the far end of the football ground that is overlooked by the White Tip. Penydarren Park was the perfect setting for the fluctuating fortunes that lay ahead for Merthyr Tydfil's football teams.

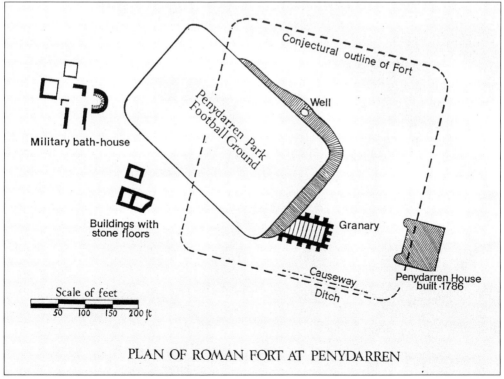

A plan of the Roman fort at Penydarren.

Merthyr Town Reserves, 1909/10. From left to right, back row: S. Smith, J. Adams (treasurer), J. Lawrence, D.H. Lewis, A.L. Jones (chairman), F. Williams, W. Jones. Second row: R. Rowlands (secretary), W. Lloyd, D. Symmonds, H. Campbell, T.J. Jones, D. Davies, A.J. Harry (trainer). Seated: A.E. Davies, J. Williams, C. Leonard, L. Duenos, G. Smith (captain).

During the first season The Tiger Inn (first right) served as a changing room for the Merthyr Town Team. Today it is the well-known Imperial Hotel.

Kruger – the Merthyr Town mascot, *c.* 1910.

David Henry Lewis, or 'Dai Henry' as he was familiarly known, was born in Dowlais and made his name with the Old Merthyr Town Reserves. He played for Merthyr from 1909 to 1913 before being transferred to Aberdare.

Jack Dodds, *c.* 1912. Jack played in every position in the forward line but was usually deployed as a very clever and speedy inside forward.

The Willows recreation ground, Troedyrhiw. Local rivals Merthyr and Troedyrhiw played many exciting derby clashes here in later years. These games were usually dour battles with few goals.

• MERTHYR TOWN, A.F.C. 1911-12 • ASS TRA

G·MACEY. W·DAVIES. C·CRAIG. D·M·LEWIS. J·WHITE. W·SAVAGE. T·JONES. W·HOLMES. (D·D. SHER) J·DODDS. H·DRAPER. G·GATES (CAPT.) F·COSTELLO. J·LOWE. F·TAYLOR.

Merthyr Town, 1911/12. In this season Merthyr won the Southern League Second Division championship, finishing above Portsmouth on goal average. The previous season they had been third in the table.

Merthyr Town	26	19	3	4	60	14	41
Portsmouth	26	19	3	4	73	20	41
Cardiff City	26	15	4	7	55	26	34
Southend United	26	16	1	9	73	24	33
Pontypridd	26	13	6	7	39	24	32
Ton Pentre	26	12	3	11	56	45	27
Walsall	26	13	1	11	44	41	27
Treharris	26	11	5	10	44	47	27
Aberdare	26	10	3	13	39	44	23
Kettering	26	11	0	15	37	62	22
Croyden Common	25	8	2	15	43	45	18
Mardy	24	6	6	12	37	51	18
Cwm Albion	22	5	1	16	27	70	11
Chesham Town	26	1	0	25	18	131	2

Cwm Albion were unable to complete their fixtures due to a coal strike affecting their area. No points were awarded for unplayed games.

Merthyr Town, 1912. From left to right, back row: Capel, -?-, -?-, -?-, Lewis, Simons, Jones, Barlow. Second row: Collins, Churchill, Holmes, Walton, Spriggs, Savage, Skinsley, Gates, Albert Fisher (manager). Front row: Taylor, Eacock, Tudor.

MERTHYR TOWN

ASSOCIATION FOOTBALL CLUB.

In contributing this, the first Annual Handbook of the Merthyr Town Football Club, I trust followers of the club will find a useful reference both as regards the players who will wear the familiar red and green jersey, and the officials who are working so diligently to provide first-class football in Merthyr. The club has been formed into a limited liability company and, fortunately, good sportsmen and a thoroughly sound body of directors have come forward, put their shoulders to the wheel and determined to run the club on sound business lines, and in the hands of such men as Messrs. Tom Elias (Chairman), Aneurin Jones, W. B. Harris, Mat DeLacey, Dr. Llewelyn Jones, Dr. Duncan and Mr. W. T. Jones, it is universally admitted that the future of the club is in safe and capable hands. We will endeavour here to emphasise the importance of every supporter of the club to become shareholders and thus have a voice in the business done. It is only by united action that we can hope for ultimate success. What such clubs as Aston Villa, Newcastle United, Everton and Bradford City, amongst others, have done, it is quite possible to do here in Merthyr, but it is only by concentrated unanimous support can we hope for success. We have a splendid fixture list, and the battles in the Southern League, Welsh League and cup ties will supply a series of exciting matches never before participated in by supporters of the club. There is no excuse for lovers of the pastime to stay away from Penydarren Park. Let us hope that when the season's record is made up it will be the brightest in the Club's history. Being but mortal, we cannot command success. In the meantime let us all have for our motto, "Forward," always bearing in mind that united we stand, divided we fall.

ALBERT FISHER,

Secretary-Manager.

The following information is from the first official handbook that Merthyr Town produced (in the 1912/13 season).

Right: Moses Russell of Merthyr was almost as legendary in pre-war soccer days as Moses of The Bible. 'Our Moses' was a tough-tackling Defender of the Soccer Faith. Take no prisoners was his commandment. When Trevor Morris, former Secretary of the Welsh FA and ex-manager of Cardiff City, heard that 1990s hard man Vinnie Jones had just stopped hanging up his Christmas stocking in case he found a spare leg in it, he replied – 'Moses of Merthyr was doing that years ago!' Shades of the late and great Trevor Richards.

Below left: A print of Merthyr Town's club colours from before the First World War. They consisted of a red shirt with a green collar, black shorts and black socks with red hoops at the top. *Below right:* F. & J. Smith cigarette card, showing Tony Burrows, the brilliant custodian. His playing days ended with the loss of an eye caused by the lace of the ball striking it from its socket – a tragic loss to a brilliant player.

LEAGUE COLOURS

B.D.V. CIGARETTES

MERTHYR TOWN

F. & J. SMITH'S CIGARETTES

MERTHYR TOWN.
T. BURROWS,
O.H.M.S.

Merthyr Town, 1912/13. From left to right, back row: C. Arthur, J. Burroughs. A. McCormach. Middle row: A. Dane, C. Gates, F. Corbett, C. Churchill, J. Dodds, C. Craig, J. Lilley, J. Pattersen. Front row: S. Reavmont, F. Taylor, T. Greaves, J. Low, W. Salkeld, J. Jeffrey, F. Jordan. Sitting: D. Neave, T. Simmonds. Insets: W. Martin, D.H. Lewis, W. Davies, J. White, A. Gimblett.

SOUTHERN LEAGUE.

			Attendance.
COVENTRY CITY ..	2	BRISTOL ROV. 2	8,000
(Feebury, Holmes.)		(Crompton, Murray.)	
CRYSTAL PALACE .	3	MERTHYR T. 1	7,000
(Williams, Smith,		(Stewart.)	
Hewitt.)			
READING	2	W. HAM U. 0	8,000
(Brown 2.)			
SOUTHAMPTON	1	PLYMOUTH A 2	14,000
(Prince.)		(Birch, Blott.)	
WATFORD	1	SWINDON 2	5,000
(Ashbridge.)		(Batty 2.)	
NORWICH CITY	2	CARDIFF C'Y. 2	6,000
(Potter, Woods.)		(Evans, Robertson.)	
GILLINGHAM	2	EXETER C'Y 0	7,000
(Gilligan, Glen.)			
NORTHAMPTON ..	5	MILLWALL .. 1	5,000
(King 2, Hughes,		(Garrett.)	
Brown 2.)			
BRIGHTON	1	Q.P. RANG'RS 0	6,000
(Miller.)			
SOUTHEND UTD. ..	3	PORTSMOUTH 2	5,000
(Wileman 2, Louch.)		(Hogg, Powell.)	

POINTS AND POSITIONS.

	P.	W.	D.	L.	Goals F.	A.	Pts.
SWINDON	8	8	0	0	24	6	16
READING	10	5	4	1	12	7	14
CRYSTAL PALACE.	9	5	3	1	13	5	13
NORTHAMPTON	9	4	3	2	17	13	11
GILLINGHAM	10	5	1	4	15	12	11
BRIGHTON & HOVE	9	3	4	2	7	6	10
PLYMOUTH A.	9	4	2	3	11	12	10
PORTSMOUTH	8	4	1	3	10	8	9
SOUTHAMPTON	9	4	1	4	13	12	9
NORWICH CITY	9	2	5	2	12	12	9
COVENTRY CITY	10	2	5	3	12	22	9
WEST HAM. U.	8	3	2	3	15	14	8
SOUTHEND U.	9	3	2	4	14	18	8
MERTHYR TOWN	8	3	1	4	5	12	7
WATFORD	11	2	3	6	14	14	7
EXETER CITY	8	2	2	4	4	6	6
MILLWALL	8	0	6	2	8	14	6
QUEEN'S PARK R.	8	1	3	4	6	11	5
CARDIFF CITY	8	1	2	5	9	12	4
BRISTOL ROVERS ..	8	1	2	5	7	12	4

Left: Johnson, the Crystal Palace goalkeeper, runs out and catches a shot from a Merthyr forward. Generous action was again typified at the Palace when, in response to an appeal, £25 was collected in aid of the Welsh Miners' Disaster Fund. This 1913 match finished Crystal Palace 3 Merthyr Town 1. *Right*: The full results of that day from the Southern League, as well as the current points and positions.

Spanish Athletic were a team consisting of Spanish immigrants living in the Dowlais and Penywern area. Many of these players lived in Alfonso Street, at that time known as 'Spaniards Row'. They played on the Bont in the Merthyr League. This photograph was taken in around 1914.

Chris Craig played in the championship side of 1911/12. He formed a part of the tenacious half-back trio of Craig, Gates and Churchill.

MERTHYR TOWN A.F.C. 1919-20

(Copyright Croci Bros)

R. WILLIAMS

564 MERTHYR TOWN

Merthyr Town, 1919/20. At the end of the First World War, Merthyr were re-elected into the Southern League First Division. Harry Hadley (ex-West Bromwich Albion) was the manager at the time.

David Rhys Williams was always known as Rhysie Tavern because he was born in the Richards Arms pub, Abercanaid. He played on the right wing for Wales on eight occasions. Rhysie played for Merthyr Town in 1919 before being transferred to Sheffield Wednesday in June 1922 for £1,000. He also played for Manchester United from 1927 until 1929.

Two
Into the Football League

Merthyr Town, *c.* 1925. From left to right, back row: Bound, Roberts, Callagan, N. Turner, Woodward, Lindon, Arblaster. Front row: Thorne, Ferrans, Phillips, Southway, E. Turner.

Merthyr Town, 1920/21. From left to right, back row: Crowe (left half), Holmes (right-back), Copeland (right-back), Lindon (goal), Ferrins (left-back), Clarke (right half), Davies (trainer). Front row: Chesser (inside left), Walker (inside right), Jennings (captain, centre half), Godfrey (centre forward), Turner (inside right), Beale (centre forward). On ground: Williams (right wing), Edwards (left wing). George Beale was transferred to Burnley and went on to get a cap for England.

QUEEN'S PARK RANGERS v. MERTHYR TOWN (L. 3).

RIGHT WING

QUEEN'S PARK RANGERS.

Goal.
1...Hill

Backs.

2...Wingrove   3...Watts

Half Backs.

4...John   5...Grant   6...O'Brien

Forwards.

7...Manning   8...Birch   9...Chandler   10...Smith   11...Gregory

LEFT WING

Referee—I. Baker.

Linesmen—Messrs. A. W. Abraham and E. J. Billiness.

**Next Match,
MILLWALL**
(L. C.)

Saturday, Feb. 5th   Kick-off 2.45.

LEFT WING

12...E. Edwards   13...Turner   14...Beale   15...Walker   16... Williams

Forwards.

17...Crowe   18...Jennings   19...Clark

Half-Backs.

20...Ferrans   21...Langford

Backs.

MERTHYR TOWN.   22...Lindon

Goal.

RIGHT WING

Programme for Queens Park Rangers v. Merthyr Town.

Miners would hurry from the day's toil at the South Tunnel, Fochriw and Bedlinog pits, travelling from work on the 'CWBS', anxious to get to the game in time for the kick-off. Coal-black faces were everywhere, with food boxes and tin jacks bobbing about as colliers rushed from Caeharris Station through the High Street in their hundreds towards Penydarren Park.

Merthyr Town A.F.C. Season 1925-1926.

Merthyr Town, 1925/26. Merthyr opened the season at Penydarren Park with Luton Town as their visitors. There were over 5,000 spectators at the match. Merthyr turned out in their new colours of red and green striped shirts and white shorts. This turned out to be a good omen as the Martyrs won the game 2-1.

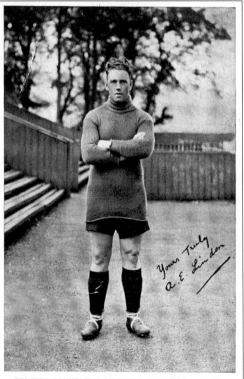

BENEFIT SOUVENIR : MERTHYR PRESENT v. PAST.
Season 1925—6.

Albert Lindon joined Merthyr from Coventry City in the season of 1920. He was appointed player-manager during the 1925 season. Later, he spent thirteen years at the Arsenal in the position of chief scout. Under his management Merthyr won the Southern League title, Southern League Cup, Welsh League title, Welsh League Cup and the South Wales & Monmouthshire Cup in one season.

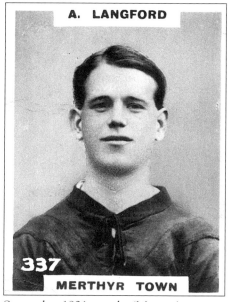

A. LANGFORD

337

MERTHYR TOWN

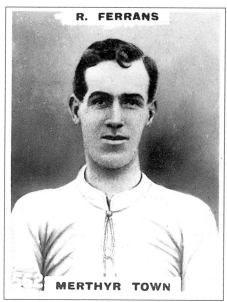

R. FERRANS

MERTHYR TOWN

September 1921 saw the 'Martyrs' in a proud position at the top of Division Three (South). The four players shown all played a major part in securing that position. They are: A. Langford (above left), R. Ferrans (above right), A.E. Lea (below left) and D.S. Nicholas (below right). Dai Nicholas – a very speedy left wing – later became a Welsh international whilst playing for Swansea Town. The *Merthyr Express* office poet was so carried away with enthusiasm that he rendered his own diagnosis of the team: 'Lindon's like old Gibraltar, like a rock he ne'er will falter; / Langford's legs are like a dancer's, beats all pirouettes and prancers, / Ferrans is a wily Scottie, Chinese say he knows a lottee; / Jennings' captaincy is clever, when he kicks it's 'now or never' / Well supporting him is Crowe a tricky bird that's 'in the know' / On his right is faithful Brown, a lad who's bound to win renown / Then the famous forward line: Reesie bach, whose footwork's fine; / Lea who soon will prove a stayer. Handsome Nicholas, always ready / Turner brave, who's ever steady, Manageered by dear old Hadley, / Who'll dare say we're doing badly?'

A. E. LEA

883

MERTHYR TOWN

D. S. NICHOLAS

338

MERTHYR TOWN

Travelling in style – the 1920s team coach.

Merthyr Town, 1928. From left to right, back row: Crewe, Page, B. Lewis, Pegler, Evans, T. Lewis. Front row: A. Morgan, Powell, Mays, Livingstone, Ford, Bishop. There were many well known teams playing with Merthyr in Division Three (South) at the time, including: Bournemouth, Brentford, Brighton, Bristol Rovers, Charlton, Coventry, Crystal Palace, Exeter City, Fulham, Gillingham, Luton Town, Newport County, Northampton, Norwich, Plymouth Argyle, QPR, Southend, Swindon Town, Torquay United, Walsall and Watford.

Three

Hard Times
in the 1930s

Heolgerrig AFC, Merthyr League Champions and Cup winners, 1939/40. From left to right, back row: Evan Phillips, Doug Morris, Thomas John Lewis, Emlyn Enoch, Brynmor Davies, Gwilym Phillips, Ambrose Thomas, Owen Davies. Gwillym Davies, Mr Cooper (secretary of the Merthyr League). Third row: Sam Wills, Evan Richards, John Pugh, Tom 'Blaencanaid' Williams, Alcwyn Williams, Evan Haines, Morgan Pedler, Dan 'Y Bobbi' Davies. Second row: John 'Y Cottage' Jones, Will 'Bach' Davies, Ossie Davies, Ly Mittell, Will John England, Bertie Abraham. Front row: Len Hamer, Ron Griffiths (mascot), Idwal Thomas. Rivalry in the Merthyr League was intense and it came as no great surprise to find that the number of famous players ending up playing in League Football had started off their careers in the Merthyr League, renowned for the quality players it produced.

OFFICIAL PROGRAMME ~ 2D.

QUEEN'S PARK RANGERS

FOOTBALL CLUB

THURSDAY
1st December, 1932

WHITE CITY STADIUM
WOOD LANE · W·12

Programme for Queens Park Rangers *v.* Merthyr Town, FA Cup first round replay. The first game at Penydarren Park had ended in a 1-1 draw. The cup tie at Merthyr was played under very bad conditions, with a gale blowing most of the time, so good football was out of the question. Amidst tense excitement the home crowd worked overtime in their endeavour to urge on the Town to score the winning goal.

The team line-ups for the game.

QUEEN'S PARK RANGERS
Royal Blue and White Hoops

Replay, 1st Rd., F.A. Cup.

Goalkeeper
1. BEECHAM

Right Back
2. BARRIE

Left Back
3. HALL

Right Half-Back
4. ADLAM

Centre Half-Back
5. ARMSTRONG

Left Half-Back
6. GOODIER

Outside Right
7. MARCROFT

Inside Right
8. GODDARD

Centre Forward
9. GOFTON

Inside Left
10. ROUNCE

Outside Left
11. BROWN

Referee :—
C. F. MOON
(Gloucester)

Linesmen :—
L. A. Martin & Q.M.S. S. Middleton
(London)   (Army)
(White & Red Flag)   (White & Blue Flag)

Outside Left
12. LOWRY

Inside Left
13. PHILLIPS

Centre Forward
14. ALDEN

Inside Right
15. MURPHY

Outside Right
16. PROTHEROE

Left Half-Back
17. JONES, G.

Centre Half-Back
18. SMITH

Right Half-Back
19. LEWIS

Left Back
20. ROGERS

Right Back
21. WILLIAMS

MERTHYR TOWN

Goalkeeper
22. WALL

Kick off 2.0.

These graphic pictures of the desolation of Penydarren Park during the Great Depression of the 1930s show the plight of Merthyr Town. The demise of the club was a real loss to the town in more senses than one.

Interviewed by a *Merthyr Express* reporter, Mr S. Richards, the secretary of the club, stated: 'Merthyr Town is finished, much as my directors regret it, they feel they have no alternative but to close down. It is impossible for them to go on running at a loss. We realise it is hopeless in existing circumstances, trying to win back Football League status. Besides there is very little prospect, with 12,000 unemployed, of the industrial situation showing any material improvement for some time'.

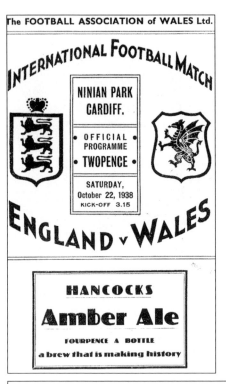

Wales *v.* England programme. Amazing crowd scenes were associated with the international between Wales and England. It is many years since a game captured the public imagination so vividly. By 3.00pm there was a record crowd of 55,000 inside the ground. The climax came when the teams entered the arena. Resounding cheers greeted the Welsh team and the mighty throng burst into a rendition of *Cwm Rhondda.*

The names and positions of the players who took part in the match.

NAMES AND POSITIONS OF PLAYERS.

Any alteration in Teams will be announced by Loud-speaker, also shown on a Board carried around the field.

Right—   ENGLAND (White)   —Left

1 WOODLEY
Chelsea

2 SPROSTON   3 HAPGOOD
Tottenham Hotspur   Arsenal (Captain)

4 WILLINGHAM   5 YOUNG   6 COPPING
Huddersfield   Huddersfield   Arsenal

7 MATTHEWS   8 ROBINSON   9 LAWTON   10 GOULDEN   11 BOYES
Stoke City   Sheffield Wed.   Everton   West Ham United   Everton

Referee :   Linesmen :

Mr. W. Hamilton (Belfast).   Wales : Mr. R. Prothero (Merthyr).

                                          England : Mr.

11 CUMNER   10 JONES (B.)   9 ASTLEY   8 JONES (L.)   7 HOPKINS
Arsenal   Arsenal   Derby Co.   Arsenal   Brentford

6 RICHARDS   5 JONES (T.)   4 GREEN
Birmingham (Captain)   Everton   Charlton Ath.

3 HUGHES   2 WHATLEY
Birmingham   Tottenham Hotspur

1 JOHN
Swansea Town

Left—   WALES (Red)   —Right

Wales beat England 4-2 in that classic soccer match at Ninian Park and the proud town of Merthyr Tydfil provided four representatives to the victorious Welsh team. All of the Welsh goals were scored by Merthyr-born players. Dai Astley of Dowlais (top left) was the hero, scoring a spectacular first goal, then baffled the whole of the English defence to score the fourth and most glorious goal of all. Idris Hopkins from Merthyr (bottom left) scored Wales's second goal, nodding it past Woodley the English goalkeeper. Bryn Jones, born in Penyard, (top right) scored the third. Dai Richards from Abercanaid (bottom right) captained the side, playing a blinder at left half. Tommy Lawton and Stanley Matthews were the English goalscorers.

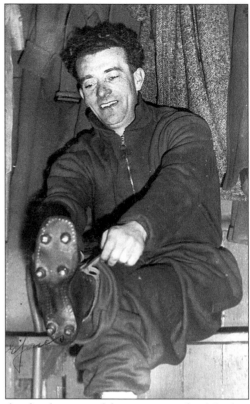

Unemployment and a terrible depression brought desolation and bitterness to the Merthyr Valley, but the Jones family of Penyard found an escape route in its remarkable gift for football. All five sons in a family of ten raised by William Daniel and Annie Jones of no. 13 Baden Terrace found their way into professional football from the coalface that each had worked in turn with their father. The eldest brother Will John 'Shoni', who turned out for Aberdare (when they were members of Football League Third Division), was soon followed by Ivor (left). Just old enough to volunteer for the army in 1917 (and having been walloped and sent back by his father after going absent), he returned legitimately and unscathed to sign for Caerphilly. Swansea had bought him within weeks. Wales capped him within months and West Bromwich Albion eventually claimed him for the delight of English crowds. The ball skills and nimbleness that gained Ivor 10 caps between 1920 and 1926 was also to be found in the third brother Emlyn (right), who weighed barely eight-and-a-half stone when he made his debut for Merthyr in 1924. Emlyn had been offered £3 a week, which his father initially declined, so the club raised their offer by 10s. Sold quickly to Bournemouth so that Merthyr could meet their close season wages, Emlyn was on the move again within six weeks after being spotted by Everton, eventually continuing his career at Southend where he became a great favourite.

A group photograph of the famous Jones family taken in 1961. From left to right, back: Bryn and Emlyn. Front: Brinley and Cliff (sons of Ivor), Ken Jones (son of Emlyn). A failed trialist at Southend, the fourth brother Bryn had wandered between Glenavon in the Irish League and Aberaman in the Welsh League, when Wolverhampton Wanderers signed him for £1,500. It proved to be the shrewdest football investment of the 1930s. Tragically, the Second World War cost youngest brother Bert his life. Good enough to be signed by Aston Villa just before the outbreak of hostilities, Bert was killed in Burma. Remarkably, the Joneses kept coming: Ken, son of Emlyn, who became chief sports writer of the *Sunday Mirror* before taking up a similar post with the *Independent*, turned professional with Southend in 1949 and subsequently turned out for Swansea and Hereford.

Bryn Jones cartoon by Lyon of the *Birmingham Gazette*.

Bryn Jones shakes the hand of King George VI before a wartime international at Wembley in 1943. Ken Jones remembers his uncle's career thus: 'Bryn was my father's brother and one of my heroes. His name won't mean much to those who follow football now. A faint echo at Highbury, a reference in the record books. But it was a different story in the summer of 1938 when Arsenal signed him from Wolves for a world record £14,000. A darting effective Welsh international inside forward, Bryn made the front pages at a time when Europe was in turmoil. Arsenal's extravagance was deplored in the House of Commons and crowds gathered in the streets of Wolverhampton threatening to burn down the goalposts at Molineux. Football saved Bryn from the darkness that only a collier knows'.

Four
Merthyr Tydfil AFC

'Jenkins the Goals' (above) tally of 53 in a season is a Southern League record that is likely to stand for a long time. Dowlais-born 'Shenkin' Powell was undoubtedly the hardest hitter of the dead ball outside the Football League. 'Shenkin' scored the two goals in Merthyr's brilliant 2-0 win over Swansea Town in the 1949 Welsh FA Cup win at Ninian Park.

Merthyr returned to the soccer scene immediately after the Second World War, this time as Merthyr Tydfil AFC (Company Law would not permit reassumption of the 'Town' suffix). The first board of directors is shown above and includes: Major Frank Crago, a director of the Rotex Company; Mr T. Longville Bowen, managing director and editor of the *Merthyr Express*; school headmaster Eddie Rowlands and E.C. Powell, a local businessman.

A rare photograph of Bryn Jones before a game at Penydarren Park in around 1945. Bryn is in the back row, third from the right.

Merthyr Tydfil goal-getter Bill Hullett (left) congratulates F. Hayward (right) on his being awarded the British Empire Medal in the New Year Honours List, 1945. This picture shows Merthyr's team before their 4-1 victory over Haverfordwest. From left to right: S. Fursland, Tommy Evans, Bert Brown, Cyril 'Tiger' Reid, Hullett, J. McNeil (player-manager), J. Pugh, Les Barlow, Dick Allen, R. Wykes, Stan Jones, The players are wearing black armbands in memory of the late Mr Ted Robbins, secretary of the Welsh Football Association.

Mr D.J. Davies presenting his magnificent charity cup to Bill Hullett, Merthyr AFC's captain, after Merthyr had defeated Lovells Athletic, the Welsh League winners, 4-0 at Penydarren Park in the game for the Mayoress' £15,000 appeal for a new Blind Institute. The game was played before a crowd of 11,000.

Bert Brown, Merthyr Tydfil AFC captain, receiving the South Wales & Monmouthshire Senior Cup from the mayor (Alderman S.O. Davies, MP) in 1946, after Merthyr had defeated Troedyrhiw 4-1 in the final in front of a 15,000 crowd at Penydarren Park.

Here they come – Bert Brown (captain and right-back), leading Merthyr's Welsh League team out at Penydarren Park in 1946. Merthyr defeated Ton Pentre 6-1 in this match.

Stan Davies joined Merthyr, his hometown, on his demobilization. He signed as a professional after a brief spell as an amateur. Stan was a pocket dynamo, scoring vital goals for Merthyr. Although he scored 28 goals in the 1953 championship season he was behind Bill Jarman (49 goals) and Trevor Reynolds (45) from all games played that season.

A gallant effort – but too late! Parsons, Merthyr's goalkeeper, makes an acrobatic attempt to stop this shot from Holman, who netted Exeter City Reserves' one and only goal in this match in November 1946. Merthyr won the game 3-1.

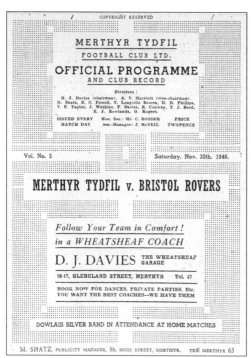

MERTHYR TYDFIL
FOOTBALL CLUB LTD.

OFFICIAL PROGRAMME
AND CLUB RECORD

Directors:
D. J. Davies (chairman), A. V. Marriott (vice-chairman),
M. Shatz, E. C. Powell, T. Longville Bowen, D. D. Phillips,
V. F. Taylor, J. Watkins, F. Davies, R. Conway, T. J. Bord,
E. J. Rowlands, O. Rogers.

ISSUED EVERY Hon. Sec.: Mr. C. ROSSER PRICE
MATCH DAY Sec.-Manager: J. McNEIL TWOPENCE

Vol. No. 5 Saturday, Nov. 30th, 1946.

MERTHYR TYDFIL v. BRISTOL ROVERS

Follow Your Team in Comfort !
in a *WHEATSHEAF COACH*

D. J. DAVIES THE WHEATSHEAF GARAGE

16-17, GLEBELAND STREET, MERTHYR Tel. 47

BOOK NOW FOR DANCES, PRIVATE PARTIES, Etc.
YOU WANT THE BEST COACHES—WE HAVE THEM

DOWLAIS SILVER BAND IN ATTENDANCE AT HOME MATCHES

M. SHATZ, PUBLICITY MANAGER, 86, HIGH STREET, MERTHYR. TEL. MERTHYR 63

4448 F.A. CUP—(1st Round)
SATURDAY, NOVEMBER 30th, 1946.
KICK-OFF 2.15 p.m.

MERTHYR TYDFIL

RIGHT LEFT
1 PARSONS
2 AVERY 3 PUGH
4 DAVIES 5 ALLEN 6 FURSLAND
7 THOMAS 8 RAYBOULD 9 HULLETT 10 POWELL 11 CRISP

Referee: Linesmen:
CAPT. HURRELL (R.A.) C. B. JACOBS (Bath).
G. EDWARDS (Hereford).

CLARK MORGAN LAMBDEN COOK PETHERBRIDGE
11 10 9 8 7
McARTHUR WARREN PITT
6 5 4
W. SMITH H. SMITH
3 2
LILLEY
1

LEFT RIGHT

BRISTOL ROVERS

SOUTHERN LEAGUE					WELSH LEAGUE				
	W.	L.	D.	Pts.		W.	L.	D.	Pts.
Chelmsford City	9	3	0	18	Gwynfi Wel.	10	2	2	22
Yeovil Town	8	3	2	18	Lovells' Ath.	9	0	0	18
Gillingham	7	3	0	14	Treharris A.	8	4	1	17
Cheltenham T.	7	3	0	14	Newport County	8	3	1	17
Colchester U.	6	4	2	14	Cardiff City	7	3	2	16
Guildford City	5	5	2	12	Ton Pentre	6	4	2	14
Gravesend & N'fld.	5	5	2	12	Milford U.	6	5	2	14
Barry Town	5	5	1	11	Barry Town	4	4	0	12
Millwall	4	6	3	11	Troedyrhiw	5	5	2	12
Exeter City	5	5	0	10	Llanelly	4	6	2	11
Merthyr Tydfil	4	4	3	11	Merthyr	4	3	3	10
Bedford Town	3	5	1	7	Abercynon	3	4	4	10
Dartford	3	8	1	7	Tredomen	4	5	2	10
Gloucester City	2	6	1	6	Ebbw Vale	4	6	1	9
Worcester City	2	6	1	5	Swansea T.	3	10	2	8
Bath City	1	7	2	4	Haverfordwest	3	7	0	6
Hereford U.	1	7	1	3	Cardiff Corries	3	7	0	6
					Caerau A.	2	8	1	5
					Nantymoel	2	10	0	4
					Garw Wel.	0	10	3	3

Merthyr Tydfil *v.* Bristol Rovers programme and teams.

In the first of two epic FA Cup ties played at Penydarren park in 1946, 'Big Bill' Hullett leads
out the team that beat Bristol Rovers 3-1.

Warren (5), the impressive Bristol Rovers captain, marshalling his defence.

Bill Hullett rises above the Rovers rearguard. His leadership in this match was, as usual, outstanding and he scored both the equalising goal and the goal that put Merthyr in front.

Lilley, the Rovers 'keeper, rushes out but loses the ball in a goalmouth scramble.

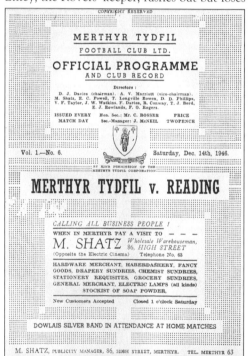

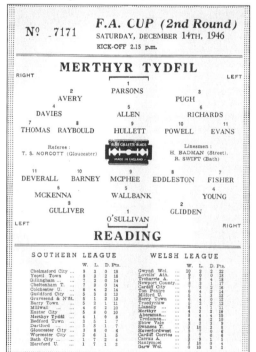

Merthyr Tydfil *v.* Reading programme cover (left) and team-sheet (right).

Merthyr's captain, Bill Hullett, shakes hands with McPhee, the Reading captain.

Merthyr under pressure from the Reading attack. The match was watched by a record-breaking crowd of 19,500.

Jenkin Powell hitting one of his 'specials'. So much of Merthyr's success came from the left wing, where Powell (of the pulverising shot) was goal king.

Merthyr Tydfil FC, January 1947. From left to right, back row: J. MacNeil (manager), Appleby, Allen, Reid, Pugh, Weale, Moore (trainer). Middle row: Thomas, Raybould, Hullett, Powell, Evans. Front row: Avery, Crisp.

Chelmsford goalkeeper Morton punches out a high one, while Raybould and Simpson wait expectantly to take advantage of any slips.

Merthyr Tydfil FC, Southern League Champions, 1947/48. This photograph of the team and officials was taken at Penydarren Park. From left to right, back row: Mr Albert Lindon (manager), Mr D.J. Davies (chairman), Mr C. Rosser (secretary), Paddy McIlvenny, Cyril Reid, Gilbert Beech, Bill Jarman, Doug Davies, Mr E. Mellors (trainer). Middle row (seated): Bob McIlvenny, Sid Howarth, Phil Tabram (captain), Trevor Richards, Stan Davies, 'Shenk' Powell. Front row (on ground): Ralph Avery, Lance Carr.

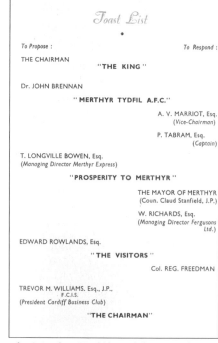

The front cover (left) and toast list (right) of the menu for Merthyr Tydfil's celebration dinner in 1948. This was laid on by the directors of the club to celebrate the outstanding achievement of winning the Southern League Championship for the first time.

Jubilant Merthyr fans show their delight as they watch their side notch up yet another win.

Merthyr Tydfil FC, winners of the Welsh Cup semi-final, 1949. From left to right, back row: E. Mellors, S. Davies, H. Lowe, C. Reid, B. Jarman, C. Beech, Bobby McIlvenny, A. Lindon (manager). Front row: R. Phillips, J. Powell, P. Tabram (captain), R. Avery, T. Richards.

Howarth's expression in this action shot is certainly not one of pleasure, and no wonder! In attempting to clear, Wright, Colchester's goalkeeper, accidentally struck the Merthyr inside-right. 'Sorry', called Wright as Howarth walked away, but the Merthyr man was too dazed to reply.

Five
Halcyon Days in the 1950s

Bill Hullett scores as Jock Stein looks on in vain during the epic FA Cup battle of Stebonheath. Football was the winner in this thrilling 5-5 FA Cup tie against Llanelli in October 1950.

Merthyr's defeat of Bangor in the Welsh Cup inspired this cartoon by 'Ralph', which appeared in the *Herald of Wales* on Saturday 11 March 1950.

Player-manager Bill Hullett being presented with the South Wales & Monmouthshire Senior Cup by Mr S.D. Lewis (vice-president of the South Wales & Monmouthshire FA) after Merthyr's 6-1 victory over Lovell's Athletic at Penydarren Park, May 1950.

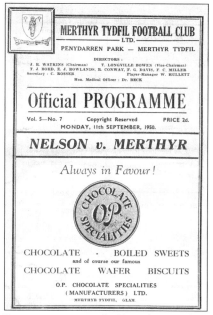

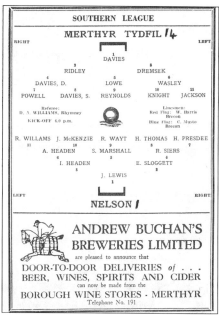

Programme cover (left) and team-sheet (right) from the Merthyr *v*. Nelson game in the Welsh League Challenge Cup game at Penydarren Park. This was a 'Knightmare' game for Nelson, with Billy Knight, the Merthyr inside left, scoring five goals. The final score was Merthyr Tydfil 14 Nelson 1.

MERTHYR BREAK ALL RECORDS WITH THAT 6-SECOND GOAL?

Feb 10ᵗ. 51.

PLAYER-MANAGER HULLETT NETS A HAT-TRICK AS FIRST DEFEAT IS AVENGED

(Merthyr 4, Cheltenham 2). Official Attendance : 4,092

[By " CANDAC "]

YESTERDAY (Thursday) Mr. E. J. Williams, of Herefordshire— the official who had charge of last Saturday's Merthyr-Cheltenham Penydarren Park game—confirmed that Merthyr's lightning goal on Saturday was hitting the back of the Cheltenham net at six seconds, which is the time also agreed by his linesmen.

If this timing is accepted, it may qualify as a new record, as the present British football record is the seven-second goal scored by Willie Sharp (Partick Thistle) against Queen's Park on Dec. 20, 1947, and equalled by Bobby Langton, playing for Preston against Manchester City on Aug. 25, 1948.

When I spoke to Mr. Alfred Dickinson (secretary), he said it was fairly certain that it established a new Southern League record.

The six-second timing may come as a surprise to many, because, quite candidly, I had clocked the goal between eight and nine seconds.

However, it was certainly a goal to remember. Hullett kicked off to Jarman, who pushed the ball to Trevor Richards (making the sixth forward). The left-half ran into an open space and sent the ball down the middle for HULLETT racing on to crack home from 20 yards with a perfect right-footer.

Left: A newspaper report of Merthyr's win over Cheltenham on Thursday 9 February 1951 – which included a goal after only six seconds! *Right:* Bill Hullett had an amazing aerial ability, seeming to 'hang' in the air above the other players. Perhaps his success could be attributed to the fact that he was schooled at Everton by the great Dixie Dean, who rated Hullett, along with Tommy Lawton, as 'head' of the class.

Merthyr Tydfil FC, Southern League Champions and Welsh Cup winners, 1950/51. From left to right, back row: T. Reynolds, D. Lloyd, R. Phillips, S. Davies, B. Hullett, R. Avery, L. Elliott. Front row: H. Lowe, B. Jarman, S. Powell, D. Davies.

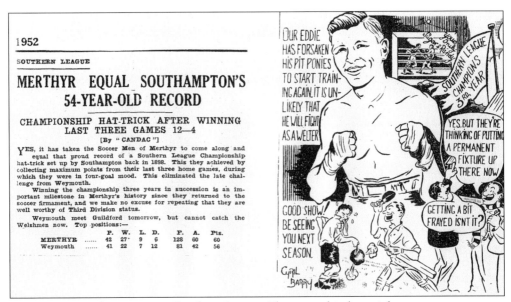

A report on Merthyr's amazing Southern League Championship hat-trick.

Bill Jarman was one of the best inside forwards in non-League football. Manager Albert Lindon secured his services from Bury when Bill Hullett moved to Cardiff City. Jarman managed an impressive tally of 53 goals in one season during his prolific career.

Why are MERTHYR TYDFIL still outside the Football League?

In spite of repeated applications Merthyr, the most successful club in the Southern League since the war, are still outside the Football League. What are their chances of admission for next season? What progress is being made with their new ground? A full investigation has been made by the EMPIRE NEWS. The findings will be published exclusively in next Sunday's issue—a special article which every South Wales Soccer fan will want to read.

Yet again the issue of Merthyr's prolonged exile from the Football League was the subject of media attention.

Left: Cartoon by Cyril Barry from December 1954. *Right*: Syd Howarth (in Aston Villa colours).

Look – no hands! Sharman, Burton's goalkeeper, fails to gather a Howells cross and Ron Skyme sets off in pursuit. Merthyr would have won the match by a comfortable margin but for a splendid performance by Sharman: two of his saves from Eisentrager (11) were miraculous. The final score was Merthyr 2 Burton 1.

Blayney, the Machynlleth goalkeeper, receives a pile-driver from the toe of a mud-stained Alan Watkins during Merthyr's 3-0 Welsh Cup win in December 1958. Alec Eisentrager is the Merthyr player just behind Watkins.

Ron Skyme charges in but Gwynn, the Llanelly 'keeper, whips the ball away, much to the relief of 'Boyo' James, the Reds centre half attempting to cover.

Merthyr centre forward Gilbert Beech (white shirt, second from the left-hand side of the photograph) heads Islwyn Jones's free-kick past the groping Gwynn for Merthyr's first goal in the 2-1 Welsh Cup win over Llanelly in January 1959.

Merthyr Tydfil FC, *c.* 1959. From left to right, back row: Brian Humphries, Brian Carpenter, Dave James, Dennis Morgan, Ronnie Skyme. Front row: Syd Howarth, Ken Parton, Harry Lowe, David Lloyd, Johnny Goggin.

Six
Sixties and Seventies

John Charles clears his lines as Newport's Willie Screen (right) attempts to get himself into a scoring position. Dilwyn John, the Merthyr goalkeeper, and full-back John Wakeham are the supporting Merthyr players. This Welsh Cup game between Newport and Merthyr took place in February 1974.

This 1960s line-up was very much a home-grown one, with all but three of the players coming from the local area. The exceptions were John Williams (from Rhymney), Graham Vearncombe (Cardiff) and Peter Roden (Swansea). From left to right, back row: David Owen (director), Tony Davies, John Williams, Graham Vearncombe, Peter Roden, Roger Williams, Gordon Evans, Howard Cadwallader. Front row: Ron Walton, David Protheroe, Viv Childerstone, Wynford Jones, Alan Owen.

RUGBY TOWN

1
J. CROSBY

2
D. FINCH

3
B. JAYES

4
B. NICHOLAS

5
A. DAVIS

6
B. JONES

9
W. HAZELDEN

7
H. MORROW

8
JACKSON

10
J. KNOX

11
G. BURROWS

TUCKER
11

DAVIES
10

WORTHINGTON
8

EDWARDS
7

McLAUGHLIN
9

WATKINS
6

WILLIAMS
5

WOOD
4

OWEN
3

PRATT
2

NORTON
1

MERTHYR TYDFIL

Colours: Black and White Shirts, Black Shorts.

Referee : E. W. Chaplin   Linesmen : C. H. MacKnight. J. H. Smith

Rugby Town *v.* Merthyr Tydfil teamsheet. This match took place in March 1964.

Merthyr Supporters' Club, *c.* 1965. From left to right, back row: David Miles, Ray Walker, Mrs Graham, Derek Phillips, May Thomas, D.M. Jones, Lyn Thomas. Front row: George Protheroe, A. Jones, Viv Caswell, Les Graham (manager), Jimmy Rees, Cyril Stuckey, Lena Davies, Gwyneth Morgan.

This is Dewi Bowen's impression of the disappearing landmarks at the Penydarren end of the ground – known as the 'magnetic end', because most of the Merthyr goals were scored there. Sadly, Penydarren Place was demolished in around 1966, at the same time as the majestic White Tip which looms in the background. A description of Penydarren Place in 1813 by J.G. Wood states that: 'The splendid mansion of Mr Samuel Homfray of Penydarren – situated upon a gently declivity – is sufficiently removed from the Town by the extent of the pleasure grounds, and contains all the conveniences and luxuries requisite for a family of wealth and importance. The gardens, which at first wore the appearance of sterility and barrenness, are now abundantly productive. The hot-houses, grape-house, etc., furnish their respective fruits in profusion and walks laid out with taste and judgement present several points from whence the silver Taff may be seen to great advantage.'

Merthyr Tydfil FC suffered a severe setback when a mystery blaze gutted the grandstand, dressing and treatment rooms and baths one Sunday morning in December 1966. One theory as to the cause of the fire is that a supporter at the match between Merthyr and Wisbech could have dropped a lighted cigarette under the grandstand floorboards. This could then have smouldered slowly until the fifty-year old stand exploded in flames. The ill-fated structure can be seen in the background of this picture, which shows Merthyr's top soccer referee, Leo Callaghan, training at Penydarren Park prior to the disaster. Penydarren Park once doubled as a greyhound stadium and some people still maintain that this was the reason the team were overlooked for admission to the Football League!

This was the grim sight at Penydarren Park after a mystery blaze gutted the grandstand and dressing rooms, destroying playing, training and physiotherapy equipment, December 1966. The club already had problems with falling gates and low finances and the Welsh FA had to step in to ease the desperate plight of the club.

Freddie and the Dreamers (along with their road managers) and Merthyr Tydfil FC taking a breather after their friendly practice game at the Park.

Merthyr Tydfil FC, September 1969. This is the team that beat Barry Town in the first qualifying round of the FA Cup. From left to right, back row: Mr Horace Thomas (chairman), Alan Wood, Brayley Reynolds, Glyn Collins, Terry Bate, Ray Hendy (captain), Jeffrey Williams, Geoff Talbot. Front row: David Collins (substitute), Gordon Evans, Brian Knight, Stan Round, Bev Watkins.

Merthyr-born referee Leo Callaghan with Everton captain Brian Labone and West Bromwich skipper Graham Williams prior to kick-off in the 1968 FA Cup final. In this match West Brom beat Everton 1-0, after extra-time, in front of a 100,000 capacity crowd. In a distinguished refereeing career, Leo officiated at five Welsh Cup finals and numerous internationals in most European countries.

Merthyr Tydfil, South Wales Senior Cup winners, 1969/70. These are the players that defeated Cardiff City in the final. From left to right, back row: Ken Tucker (manager), John Williams, Brian Davies, Howard Cadwallader, Graham Vearncombe, Pat Murphy, Peter Roden, Ieuan Evans (trainer). Front row: W. Rees, Viv Childerstone, Brayley Reynolds, Clive Lloyd, Malcolm Gilligan.

Merthyr Tydfil FC, 1970. From left to right, back row: David Owen (chairman), Ieuan Evans (trainer), Les Harris, Dilwyn John (player-coach), Pat Murphy, Colin Crotty, Mike Hayes, John Bird, Brian Davies (substitute), Maldwyn Davies (managing director). Front row: Harry Robinson, Alan Wilkins, Howard Madley (captain), Malcolm Gilligan, Terry Collins.

GERRY HITCHENS
Aston Villa

Having started his career with Kidderminster Harriers, Gerry Hitchens played for Aston Villa, Atalanta and Cardiff City. He played for England in the 1962 World Cup in Chile and won 7 international caps. He signed for Merthyr on a free transfer from Worcester City.

A superb goalscorer, Gordon Davies played many splendid games for Merthyr and was a key figure in their great non-League cup run of 1977/78. Gordon went on to make the breakthrough into League football at Fulham and, in October 1990, overtook the legendary Johnny Haynes to establish himself as Fulham's record goalscorer. Gordon won a total of 18 caps for Wales.

Ray Best and Clive Lloyd in action for Merthyr against Banbury United at Penydarren Park in 1971.

Merthyr Tydfil before their friendly with Division Two Bristol City in 1973. From left to right, back row: Frank Hagerty, Peter Thomas, Alan Smith, Mel Nurse, Carl Slee, Stuart Meek, John Charles (manager), Dilwyn John, Jim Hobby, Ieuan Evans (trainer). Front row: Barrie Jones, Derek Bryant, Nick Deacy, Doug Rosser (captain), Paul Caviel, George Young.

John Charles and a willing band of helpers doing promotional work at the Hoover Sports Ground, Merthyr Tydfil, August 1973.

John Charles, soccer's 'Gentle Giant', was appointed manager of Merthyr Tydfil AFC in January 1972. Under his guidance Merthyr reached the second round proper of the FA Cup for only the third time in their history. In a dazzling career John had played for Leeds United, Juventus and Wales. Whilst in Italy he had scored 28 goals for Juventus in one season, having struck up a devastating partnership with Argentinian international Omar Sivori. Many people rate him the greatest British-born player of all time.

The old and new faces at Penydarren appear to be enjoying their training session in September 1978. The 'wheelbarrow' pairs are, from left to right: Paul Caviel and Mickey Dicks, Gerry Ingram and Alan Sullivan, Don Payne and Peter Lewis.

Merthyr Tydfil AFC, 1979. From left to right, back row: Mark Fleet, Alan Sullivan, Paul Caviel, Chris Holvey, Don Payne, M. Carter, Ieuan Evans (trainer), Frank Hagerty. Front row: Ray Pratt, John Wakeham, Dave Jones, Doug Rosser, Ian Docherty, M. Lenihan.

Seven
The Uneasy Eighties

Merthyr Tydfil AFC, 1986. From left to right, back row: Frank Hagerty (coach), Chris Baird, Roger Mullen, Steve Westerberg, Anthony Hopkins, Gary Wager, Geoff Miller, Gerry Byrne, Lyn Jones (manager). Front row: Paul Giles, Steve James, Ceri Williams, Chris Holvey, David Webley, Wynford Hopkins.

Derek Elliott, Merthyr Tydfil's popular winger, was voted Player of the Season 1980/81 by the board of directors. The presentation was made by vice-chairman Jackie James.

Merthyr Tydfil FC, 1980. From left to right, back row: Frank Hagerty, Doug Rosser (manager), Ian Docherty, Alan Sullivan, Chris Holvey, Mark Harmon, Jeff Shaw, Paul Caviel, Phil Green, R. Batt, Ieuan Evans (trainer). Front row: Clive Ayres, Mike Ellery, Cyril Stuckey (chairman), Peter Jones, Keith Stimpson

Merthyr Tydfil FC, 1982. From left to right, back row: Frank Hagerty, David Williams, John Williams, Mike Coslett, Alan Meacham, Mike Carter, Derek Elliott, Chris Holvey. Front row: Anthony James, Ian Docherty, Ian Love, Cyril Stuckey (chairman), Jackie James (vice-chairman), Peter Jones, Phil McNeil.

Keith Pontin (white shirt with thin black stripes) photographed in action against Barry Town. Signed for Merthyr in 1983, he stayed with the club until 1986. Keith played over 250 games for Cardiff City and was capped twice for Wales.

Merthyr Tydfil AFC, *c*. 1983. From left to right, back row: Frank Hagerty, Chris Williams, John Allchurch, Keith Pontin, Wayne Jones, Barry Vassallo, Chris Holvey, Mick Carter, Ieuan Evans. Front row: Phil Fisher, John Williams, Peter Jones, Kyle Holmes, Brian Davies

Ian Love's left foot drives the ball goalwards to score in Barry's 3-2 win over Merthyr during a 1984 FA Cup tie. The players in the photograph are, from left to right: Peter Jones, Phil Green, Ian Love and Keith Pontin. All of them played for Merthyr at one time or other.

Merthyr Tydfil represented the Southern League in the Anglo-Italian tournament in April 1986. The squad that competed was comprised of, from left to right, back row: Frank Hagerty (coach), W. Jones, A. Hopkins, A. Beattie, S. Westerburg, G. Miller, G. Wager, R. Mullen, John Charles (special guest), T. Collins (director), L. Jones (manager). Front row: A. James, C. Baird, C. Williams, C. Holvey, S. James, D. Webley, W. Hopkins.

John Charles and Gary Wager on the training ground in Italy. The 'Gentle Giant' is held in high esteem in Italy and it was a fine gesture by Merthyr to invite him along with the team.

Merthyr Tydfil AFC 'Exclusive 500', December 1986. Ted Rowlands MP is being enrolled into the club by Merthyr's chairman, Mr J. Reddy, whilst vice-chairman Mr Gerry Collins and 'Santa' Bob Latchford look on.

After scoring the first goal against Bilston on Easter Monday 1987, Dai Webley – Merthyr's goalscoring ace – is carried off with a bad knee injury. The club's top goalscorer in the Southern League missed the next four fixtures and only returned (heavily strapped) to try and give some bite to the attack for the last league fixture of the season against VS Rugby. He was unable to add to his tally of 53 goals.

Eight

Two Days in May 1987

Bob Latchford towering high above the Newport defence as a stout-hearted performance by a marvellous team of Merthyr heroes brought the Welsh Cup back to Penydarren Park and the Borough of Merthyr for the first time in thirty-six years.

MERTHYR TYDFIL A.F.C. LTD

PENYDARREN PARK
MERTHYR TYDFIL

Official Souvenir Yearbook
1986/87

Merthyr Tydfil A.F.C. leave for their visit to Bangor City
(2nd Leg of the Welsh Cup)

UP FOR THE CUP

Merthyr Tydfil AFC's *Official Souvenir Yearbook* for the 1986/87 season.

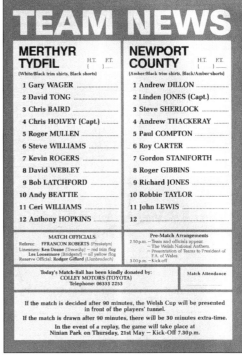

The front and reverse cover of the Merthyr *v.* Newport County 1987 Welsh Cup final programme.

The team that did the town of Merthyr Tydfil proud, before the first game at Ninian Park – a 2-2 draw. From left to right, back row: Lyn Jones, Anthony Hopkins, Andy Beattie, Steve Williams, Gary Wager, Bob Latchford, Roger Mullen, Kevin Rogers, Frank Hagerty. Front row: Ceri Williams, Chris Holvey, Chris Baird, Dave Webley, David Tong.

Big Bob Latchford in a mighty tussle with the Newport defence. Bob was a vastly experienced centre forward who had played for Everton and Birmingham City, as well as being capped 12 times for England in the 1970s.

The equaliser! Latchford cracks the ball into the net to score Merthyr's first goal.

David Webley (8) forces the game into extra-time as he beats the County defence to the ball to level the scores with Merthyr's second goal.

A day we'll never forget – jubilant crowd scenes at Ninian Park.

Ceri Williams has the Newport defence on the run.

David Webley takes a tumble over Andy Dillon as the Newport goalkeeper dives bravely at his feet. Bob Latchford is the Merthyr player in close attendance.

Spot on for Europe: Chris Baird scored the penalty that made it a night of glory for Merthyr. Chris looked back on that vital score and said, 'I regarded myself as the club's penalty-taker, there was no way I was going to miss the spot-kick; I wanted to give my side the lead'. Cool words from an ice-cool player.

Celebrating that memorable night at Ninian Park, the team proudly wearing their *Merthyr Express*-sponsored shirts.

'Up for the Cup' – included in the photograph are, from left to right: Howard King, Peter Jones, Anthony Hopkins, Kevin Rogers, Ken Tucker (secretary), John Reddy (chairman) and Paul Owen (director).

The Merthyr team touring the town after the memorable 1-0 Welsh Cup triumph over Newport County at Ninian Park, Cardiff.

Celebrations in the Merthyr dressing room after the Martyrs had beaten Newport County in the replay of Welsh Cup final.

Lyn Jones celebrates on the balcony of the Town Hall. Sheer satisfaction, sheer joy, sheer delight – call it what you will – the Merthyr manager holds up the Welsh Cup in triumph and shows by his big smile that he's 'Over the Moon'.

'Man in the middle' Howard King was the reserve referee at England's centenary match against the Rest of the World at Wembley in 1987. At this time, Howard was the fund-raising consultant with the Martyrs and is pictured here between the great Diego Maradona and Bryan Robson, the England captain.

Nine
Arrivederci Atalanta

The opposing captains meet in the centre circle: Andy Beattie of Merthyr and Glenn Stromberg of Atalanta shake hands before Merthyr's unforgettable 2-1 victory.

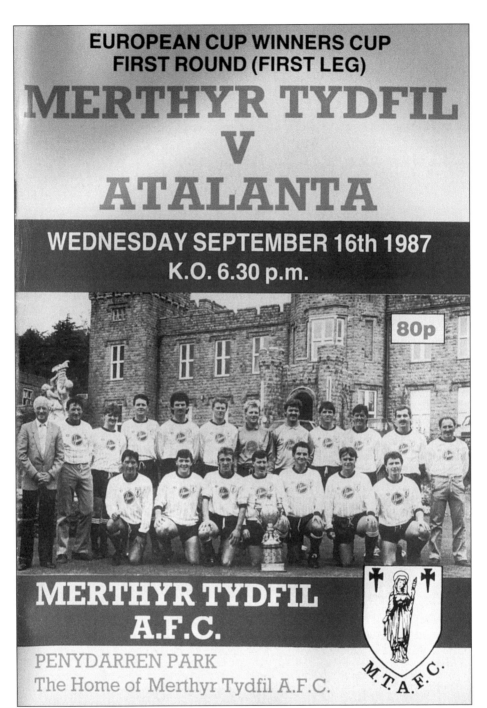

EUROPEAN CUP WINNERS CUP
FIRST ROUND (FIRST LEG)

MERTHYR TYDFIL
V
ATALANTA

WEDNESDAY SEPTEMBER 16th 1987
K.O. 6.30 p.m.

80p

MERTHYR TYDFIL A.F.C.

PENYDARREN PARK
The Home of Merthyr Tydfil A.F.C.

The front cover of the Merthyr *v.* Atalanta match programme. Atalanta Football Club are based in Bergamo, a city in Lombardy situated at the feet of Alps on the edge of the Po Valley in Northern Italy. The capacity of their ground, the Stadio Comunale, is 40,000 and the club was formed in 1907. Atalanta had reached the Italian Cup final the season before, losing both legs to Diego Maradona's Napoli. However, Napoli had also won the Championship and so entered the European Cup, leaving the place in the Cup Winners Cup to Atalanta.

The skilful Swedish international Glenn Stromberg is beaten in the air by Roger Mullen. Glenn admitted that the Italian club's fans did not take kindly to the first-leg defeat.

A cartoon of Merthyr celebrating their great victory over Atalanta.

Merthyr's goalie, Gary Wager, reserved one of his finest performances for the glorious first-leg victory over Atalanta at Penydarren Park.

Skipper Andy Beattie heading for goal. Andy and Kevin Rogers were the midfield masters against an Atalanta side that had been assembled at a cost of £1.5 million.

Atalanta's Icardi (8) and goalkeeper Piotti are helpless as Kevin Rogers' free-kick goes in for Merthyr's first goal.

Ottorino Piotti is beaten again as Merthyr's Ceri Williams scores the winning goal for the Martyrs. The greatest night in Merthyr's history will long be remembered and, as Max Boyce would proudly say, 'I was there'!

Chris Williams (right), Wayne Jones (centre) and Ceri Williams seated on the hotel roof on the morning of the match. The medieval centre of Bergamo is in the background. A comparison of the two cultures was made by Mario Basini of the *Western Mail*: 'My home town of Merthyr may be a bit short on medieval churches and renaissance masterpieces, but when it comes to a passionate commitment to its own patch of the globe it can match the legendary pride of the Italians in their native land any day'.

Merthyr Tydfil AFC, before the match in Bergamo. From left to right, back row: Rogers, Mullen, Wager, Evans, Chris Williams. Front row: Baird, French, Tong, Beattie, Ceri Williams, Webley.

A giant Atalanta flag in the club colours covered the whole section of terracing at one end of the ground in Bergamo.

Icardi gets in a goal-bound shot, despite the presence of Evans (5) and Kevin Rogers.

David Webley and Nigel French looking for an elusive equalising goal. The Martyrs were beaten by two disputed goals, scored by Atalanta in the first half.

Merthyr supporters in Bergamo preparing for the big kick-off. At the end of the game Italian supporters gathered in a spirit of friendship, swapping scarves and flags with their Merthyr counterparts before applauding them on to their coaches.

Garlini (on the ground) heads just wide, giving Gary Wager and Chris Baird a scare.

Striker Garlini, who Atalanta had bought for £500,000 from Inter Milan, puts the Italian side ahead after 16 minutes. Although Atalanta won 2-0, the proud Penydarren Park part-timers went out of the cup with a glorious 3-2 aggregate defeat, returning to Merthyr promising they would return to European football in the near future.

Merthyr Manager Lyn Jones looks pensive as the European dream comes to an end.

Ten

Champions Again

Merthyr Tydfil AFC, December 1987. From left to right, back row: Wynford Hopkins (coach), Kevin Rogers, Anthony Hopkins, Roger Mullen, Gary Wager, Bob Latchford, David Webley, Lyn Jones (manager), Frank Hagerty (trainer). Front row: Steve Williams, Andy Beattie, Chris Holvey, Chris Baird, David Tong, Peter Jones.

Merthyr put the disappointment of their exit from Europe behind them as they demolished poor Rushden Town 11-0 in the Beazer Homes Midland Division in October 1987. Chris Williams chalked up a personal milestone by scoring six goals in the match.

John Reddy, the Merthyr chairman (left), Leo Callaghan's widow Doreen and Peter Jackson at the opening of the Leo Callaghan Suite at Penydarren Park in November 1987.

Two photographs of the Martyrs' magnificent 2-0 Welsh Cup fourth round win over Swansea at the Vetch Field in January 1988. *Above*: Defensive action with David Tong on the goal-line as 'keeper Wayne Jones looks on anxiously. *Below*: Phil Green, Phil Evans and Roger Mullen battle for possession against the Swansea attack.

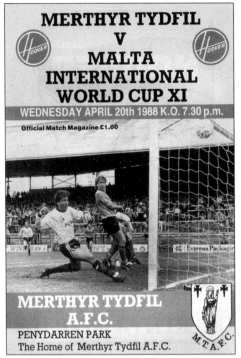

Left: The front cover of the programme for Merthyr Tydfil *v.* Malta International. *Right:* Chris Williams misses a golden opportunity.

A brilliant save from the Maltese goalkeeper did not prevent Merthyr winning this prestigious fixture 2-1.

Chairman John Reddy presents David Webley with a commemorative tankard following his hat-trick against Corby Town in September 1988.

Peter Jones (centre) played consistently for Merthyr over a number of seasons. A tenacious tackler, he has appeared for the Welsh non-League side.

Andy Beattie, the Merthyr captain, being presented with the Championship Cup by Mr John Eastment at the end of the 1988/89 season.

Merthyr Tydfil AFC celebrating the championship win in May 1988. From left to right, back row: Lyn Jones (manager), Chris Baird, Ceri Williams, Paul Giles, Phil Evans, David Webley, Kevin Rogers, Roger Mullen, David Tong, Gary Wager, Steve Williams, Frank Hagerty, Chris Holvey. Front row: John Eastment (Beazer League chairman), Wayne Jones, Andy Beattie, Phil Green, Chris Williams, Peter Jones.

Delighted Merthyr players watch Paul Giles almost overpower goalscorer David Webley, following the Merthyr man's second goal against Crawley.

Smiles all around as Merthyr skipper Andy Beattie (left) and Kevin Rogers lift the Beazer Homes Premier Division League Shield in May 1989.

Ian Thompson scoring in the South Wales Senior Cup final first-leg against Barry Town. The game at Penydarren Park finished 2-0 to The Martyrs.

Merthyr ending their season in style, adding another trophy to their impressive list of recent achievements by clinching the South Wales Senior Cup at Barry, winning 3-2 on aggregate.

Eleven

The GM Vauxhall Conference

Mark Tucker scores against Bath in a 1-1 draw at Penydarren Park in 1992. Mark scored many spectacular goals in his time with The Martyrs.

Paul Giles, Merthyr's mercurial flanker, scored Merthyr's first goal in the GM Vauxhall Conference – against Sutton United – in August 1989.

Ceri Williams, the highly talented striker, seen here scoring one of his many goals for Merthyr since joining the club on New Year's Day 1986.

Phil Green's superb diving header finds the back of the net for Merthyr's third goal in their 4-2 replay win over Dulwich Hamlet in November 1989.

Long-serving defender Chris Holvey walking out onto Penydarren Park with the Watford captain for his well-deserved testimonial match in December 1989.

Paul Giles (kneeling) celebrates after scoring the third goal in the 3-0 victory at Welling in March 1990. Jeff Lissaman is the Merthyr player on the left.

ENGLAND v WALES at Merthyr Tydfil 6th March 1990

David Howell and Russell Lewis meet before the recent England visit to play Wales at Merthyr Tydfil

WALES 0 ENGLAND 0

at Merthyr Tydfil on Tuesday 6th March 1990

THERE is no doubt that Penydarren Park, the home of Merthyr Tydfil, the home of impressive football grounds in the country. This little Welsh stadium is ideal for the size of attendances likely to be attracted to matches at Merthyr and could hardly be better equipped.

Since qualifying to play in the European Cup Winners Cup, Chairman John Reddy and his back-up team have transformed the ground into the perfect stadium with safe, clean and smart terraces, new seating, a spacious stand, social facilities for all (public bar, members bar, players bar, boardroom with restaurant and chairmans suite). There is also a lavishly furnished function room and well catered tea bars on both sides of the ground for use during the match.

So it was understandable that this years Wales v England semi-professional match should be played at Merthyr and as the local team were in the middle of a purple patch and the playing surface was also in peak condition a good attendance of over 2,000 saw a spirited contest fought out with a lot of neat approach work

flowing across the park. Unfortunately neither side seemed very willing to commit much support for their front runners thus enabling two well organised defences to remain on top for most of the evening.

Englands attack of Mark Carver and Steve Butler who had been so impressive last season were no longer available. Mark out through injury (as was Robbie Cooke) and Steve in the Barclays League with Maldstone but Paul Furling with only one England cap teamed up with debutant John Askey and although they really needed more support, Paul impressed throughout and John was fast and mobile and will certainly have benefited from the experience. It was good to see Noel Ashford back in the England side and what a fine performance he gave as he covered every blade of grass in his efforts to back the defence with attack.

There were certainly no England disappointments individually, only the feeling this time were always a little short of manpower when going forward. An excellent back four were well covered by Glenn Skivington as sweeper and Andy Pape was hardly troubled.

The Welsh included their countrymen based in England for the first time and this brought in the very solid central defenders Russell Lewis (Kettering Town) and Elfyn Edwards (Macclesfield Town) who are 'uncompromising' to say the least. The home side, with their abundance of Merthyr players full of confidence, didn't

try to match England for approach play and gave their three first half strikers (all central players) service from the mid-field.

In the second-half they introduced a variation by using the wing-men and David Webley just shot wide after an excellent move.

Indeed England also created their best chances with some speedy attacks down the flanks with the variation of chips over the big Welsh defenders from which Paul Furling with closest just after half-time.

In summing up, both sides will be a little disappointed with their 'fire power' and England certainly missed Mark Carver's experience in this facet of their game. Wales have failed to score in the last three games in the series but at least England are building up an understanding again and their games in Southern Ireland, in Dublin (Tolka Park, May 25, 7.30pm) and Cork (Turners Cross, May 27, 3.00pm) should see the team benefiting from the two games in the last ten days.

J.W.

WALES		ENGLAND	
1	Gary Wager (Merthyr Tydfil)	1	Andy Pape (Enfield)
2	Chris Evans (Bangor City)	2	Paul Shirtliff (Boston United)
3	Nigel Stevenson (Merthyr Tydfil)	3	Paul Bancroft (Kidderminster H)
4	Elfyn Edwards (Macclesfield Town)	4	Dave Howell (Enfield)
5	Russel Lewis (Kettering Town)	5	Glenn Skivington (Barrow)
6	Mark Tucker (Merthyr Tydfil)	6	Phil Gridelet (Barnet)
7 (14)	Craig Gill (Yeovil Town)	7	John Askey (Macclesfield Town)
8	David Webley (Merthyr Tydfil)	8	Steve Harlow (Macclesfield Town)
9 (13)	Graham Bennett (Marine)	9	Paul Furlong (Enfield)
10	Andy Beattie (Merthyr Tydfil)	10	Noel Ashford (Redbridge Forest)
11 (15)	Phil Williams (Cheltenham Town)	11	Gary Simpson (Altrincham)
12	Trevor Ball (Bangor City)	12	John McKenna (Boston United)
13	Paul Giles (Merthyr Tydfil)	Subs	Paul Watts (Redbridge Forest)
14	Phil Green (Merthyr Tydfil)	(not used)	Paul Rogers (Sutton United)
15	Steve Williams (Merthyr Tydfil)		Efan Ekoku (Sutton United)
16	Ray John (Barry Town)		Steve Brooks (Cheltenham Town)

Left: Wales 0 England 0 in the non-League international match played at Penydarren Park. Merthyr supplied eight of the players as well as manager Lyn Jones, coach Wynford Hopkins and trainer Frank Hagerty. *Right:* The line-ups for the Wales v. England game.

TV personality Russell Grant presents David Webley with a tankard for his hat-trick against Welling United. Chairman John Reddy, vice-chairman Lyn Mittell and local MP Ted Rowlands complete this line-up in April 1990.

Merthyr's prolific scorer Dai Webley scores against Welling at Penydarren Park in 1990.

Phil Green and Roger Mullen challenge the Stafford Rangers defence in Merthyr's 4-3 victory at Penydarren park in April 1990.

Ian Thompson scores the equaliser against Boston to make the score 1-1. The final score in this 1989/90 season match was 2-2.

Penydarren Park was the venue for the under-21 international between Wales and Poland in May 1990.

Action from the Poland game. Chris Coleman, Gary Speed and Simon Dyer all played a part in the superb Welsh victory.

The Martyrs line up before rocking the Red Star Roadshow with a vintage performance against one of Europe's best teams.

Red Star lined up at Penydarren Park with six Yugoslavian internationals in their side. The following season Red Star won the European Champions Cup, defeating Marseille of France in a penalty shoot-out. Ten of the side that played at the Park were in the Champions Cup winning team.

Yugoslav internationals Refic Sabandzovic (left) and Robert Prosinecki sign a few footballs just before Merthyr's pre-season friendly with Red Star Belgrade.

Red Star on the attack during the explosive encounter at Penydarren Park. Howard King, the FIFA referee, sent off two Yugoslav players in this action-packed 1-1 draw. Robert Prosinecki scored a goal out of the top draw for Red Star, with substitute Jason Gummer finding the net for the Martyrs.

Ian Thompson battles away in a disappointing 2-0 defeat away against Stafford Rangers in 1990. Ian and his striking partner David Webley formed a lethal combination up front with their prolific goal-scoring feats.

Yet another trophy for his cabinet – John Reddy presents Dai Webley with this trophy for his superb hat-trick against Cardiff City after a remarkable 4-1 victory, with Merthyr completely outplaying Cardiff in a thrilling Welsh Cup tie at Ninian Park.

Merthyr Tydfil *v.* CSKA Moscow programme cover and teams list. The match took place on 22 November 1990.

CSKA Moscow team group. Formed in April 1923, CSKA are sponsored by the Russian Army and have been champions of the Soviet League on six occasions and have won the Cup Winners Cup four times.

Merthyr Tydfil AFC, 1990. From left to right, back row: Phil Green, Steve Williams, Jeff Lissaman, Terry Boyle, Kevin Rogers, Paul Sanderson. Middle row: Chris Holvey, Russell Lewis, Gary Wager, Ian Thompson, Nigel Stevenson. Front row: Paul Giles, David Webley, Andy Beattie, Ceri Williams, Mark Tucker.

Lyn Jones' record is second to none in non-League football. Under his leadership Merthyr won the Welsh Cup in 1987 and played against Atalanta in the European Cup Winners tournament. This was followed by the winning the Beazer Homes League and the Premier Division championship and then promotion into the GM Vauxhall Conference. His attacking style also won the Martyrs three Welsh Senior Cup wins. Success was synonymous with Lyn Jones!

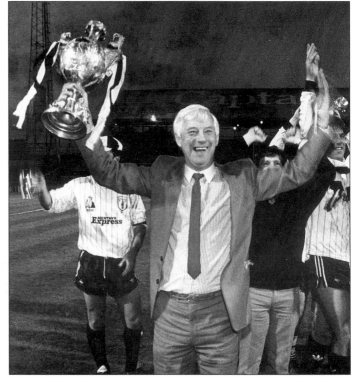

Merthyr Tydfil AFC, Middlesex Charity Shield winners, 1991. The Martyrs won the trophy by defeating Hayes 2-1.

Two local champions of the boxing world were present at the opening of the Bill Hullett Suite at Penydarren Park in December 1991. Eddie Thomas MBE (left) was British, European and Empire Champion and one of the finest welterweights Britain has ever produced. Howard Winston MBE was World Champion. He had won this honour by beating Japanese featherweight Seki at the Royal Albert Hall in June 1968.

The Merthyr side that played in the final Welsh League game. Saturday 4 May 1991 will go down as a sad day in the history of Merthyr Tydfil AFC, as the club played their last Welsh League game at Penydarren Park. Following the resumption of football after the Second World War, crowds of 4,000-5,000 were a common sight at Penydarren Park. Indeed, in October 1945 a crowd of 10,000 attended the local derby with Troedyrhiw. The Martyrs won their last Welsh League game, against Ynysybwl, 3-2.

Tommy Hutchison won 17 caps for Scotland, making his debut for Alloa in 1968. Whilst playing against Farnborough in 1992, he scored one of the most spectacular goals ever seen at Penydarren Park. Tommy was a great favourite with the Merthyr crowd.

Merthyr Tydfil AFC, GM Vauxhall Conference, 1991/92. From left to right, back row: S. Hookings, T. Boyle, G. Wager, I. Thompson, G. Wood, E. Chiverton, D. Webley. Middle row: F. Hegarty (trainer), R. James, C. Hemming, R. Lewis, C. Summers, T. Hutchison (coach), M. Williams, C. Williams, W. Hopkins (manager). Front row: P. Evans, M. Pengelly, C. Thomas, K. Rogers, A. Beattie, J. Morgan, D. Burrows.

There were five new signings for the 1992 season, from left to right: Mark Davies, Craig Gill, Des Trick, Marc Coates and Adrian Needs.

Robbie James joined Merthyr from Cardiff City as a player-manager in October 1993 and, after leaving the managerial position in April 1994, stayed on as a player until he joined Barry Town in September of that year. Tragically, Robbie died of a heart attack in 1998. Merthyr fans held a minute's silence for Robbie during the home game against Burton and he will be sadly missed by both his family and the world of football.

A happier occasion at the Park, from left to right: David D'auria, Kevin Rogers, Mark Tucker, Eston Chiverton, Tommy Hutchison, Mark Williams.

Twelve

Back to the Beazer

Gareth Abraham holding the runner-up trophy for the European Small Nations tournament held in Malta. Gareth has been a pillar of strength in the Merthyr defence and is today playing as well as ever.

Cyril 'Tiger' Reid (left) was a goalkeeping legend and Harry Lowe (right) a cultured centre half. Both of these players from 1950s Merthyr sides are photographed enjoying a visit to their old football field.

Ken Gunter became chairman of Merthyr Tydfil AFC on 20 December 1995. Ken envisaged many changes taking place and his ambition was for the club to reach Conference status again. Unfortunately, Ken retired due to ill health in 1997. The above photograph shows Ken enjoying the company of his granddaughter at Penydarren Park.

MERTHYR TYDFIL
v.
SHEFFIELD WEDNESDAY

MARK PEMBRIDGE

TUESDAY, 12th NOVEMBER, 1996
Kick off 7.30 p.m.

Souvenir Programme: **£1.50**

Merthyr Tydfil *v.* Sheffield Wednesday souvenir programme cover. Sheffield Wednesday were a class act, beating The Martyrs 3-0 in the friendly game played at Penydarren Park. Wednesday players Regi Blinker and Orlando Trustful were a joy to watch, each scoring a goal in front of 2,327 fans – the biggest attendance for years. Locally-born Welsh international Mark Pembridge captained the Wednesday team.

Left: Leyton Orient *v.* Merthyr Tydfil programme cover. *Right:* Paul Evans celebrates after scoring the opening goal for The Martyrs.

Greg Downs 'leads the line' as Merthyr nearly cause an upset in the 1996 FA Cup first round tie, eventually losing 2-1 to the London opposition.

Colin Addison had a successful career as a player and as a manager: playing for Arsenal and Hereford United. During his managerial career he was involved with Hereford, Athletico Madrid and Merthyr on two occasions. Colin's second spell as Merthyr's manager saw the Martyrs narrowly missing out on winning the league title that would have taken them back to the Vauxhall Conference.

Super striker Sam Bowen scored an amazing five goals against Gravesend and Northfleet on his league debut for Merthyr in March 1997.

The game of the 1997/98 season saw Merthyr beat their promotion rivals, Forest Green Rovers, 4-0 at Penydarren Park. *Above:* Merthyr defender Neil O'Brien rises above the Forest Green defence to score the first goal with a header after 72 seconds. *Below:* Anthony Jenkins scores Merthyr's third goal on a snowy Easter Monday. However, despite the impressive victory at the Park, Forest Green became Dr Martens League Premier Division champions at the end of the season.

Merthyr Tydfil AFC, 1997/98. From left to right, back row: Colin Loss, Tony Rees, Dean Clarke, Ian French, Neil O'Brien, Gary Wager, Shaun Chapple, Dave Barnhouse, Anthony Rivett, Chris Summers, Colin Addison (manager). Front row: Anthony Jenkins, Ian Mitchell, Cohen Griffiths, Gareth Abraham, Roger Gibbins, Roy Jordan, Terry Green, Darren Porretta.

Ian Mitchell scored 30 goals for Merthyr in 1997/98 and claimed the Adidas Predator Dr Marten's Goalscorers Award. Ian joined Merthyr in 1994 and has served the club well.

In August 1998, The Martyrs witnessed a managerial merry-go-round at Penydarren Park, beginning with Colin Addison ending his association with the club. John Lewis (shown above) was appointed as his successor, although he parted company with the club on 2 December 1998. Eddie May was introduced to the players as the new manager on 3 December and he stayed in the post into 1999. Roger Gibbins was appointed in March and he soon secured the club's league position. Merthyr will certainly be aiming for the Conference in the near future!

Merthyr Tydfil AFC, 1998. From left to right, back row: John Lewis (manager) Ray John, Craig Evans, Mark Williams, Eston Chiverton, Jamie Harris, Neil Thomas, Craig Lima, Ben Graham, Shaun Chapple, David Giles (coach). Front row: Paul Giles (assistant manager), Cohen Griffiths, Gary Shephard, Gareth Abraham (captain), Adrian Needs, Rob King, Andrew Needs (physiotherapist). This photograph of the team was taken before their 1-0 win over Hastings.

Scorer Gary Shephard wheels away from the Nuneaton goal after celebrating Merthyr's second goal. Merthyr won the game 2-1, with Nuneaton going on to become champions of the Dr Martens Premier Division 1998/99.

Merthyr Tydfil Football Club was privileged to hold the last Welsh Cup final of the twentieth century between Inter Cable Tel and Carmarthen Town. Inter Cable Tel won the game at Penydarren Park 4-2 on penalties. This lovely old ground was once the home of many exciting Merthyr teams and players. Great names, such as Bill Hullett, Moses Russell, Shenkin Powell, John Charles, Harry Lowe, Dai Webley, Alan Sullivan, Dai Lloyd, Stan Round, Ceri Williams and the rest, are in the atmosphere at Penydarren Park and they will always hold a distinctive place in our memories.

Kevin Rogers scores number one against Atalanta – one of the most important goals ever seen at Penydarren Park.

Acknowledgements

I wish to thank the following individuals, newspapers and organisations for their help and assistance in making this book possible and for the use of their photographs, collected over a number of years.

Merthyr Tydfil Public Libraries, *Merthyr Express*, *Western Mail and Echo*, Aerofilms Limited, *Swansea Evening Post*, All Sport Photographic Limited, S4C and 'Urdd Gobaith Cymru', Rugby Town AFC, Leyton Orient AFC, Colin Parker, Viv Bayliss, Frank Hagerty, David Miles, Terry Collins, John Reddy, Wayne Hodgkins, Howard King, Dave Webb, Ken Tucker, Philip Howells, Les Williams, John Yates, Gordon Caldicott, Dave Williams, Ian Carbis, Nino Cassotti, Phil Davies, Tony Barette, Ceri Stennett, Robert Prosser, Mark Powell, Miss G. Powell, Merthyr Tydfil AFC, *Birmingham Post and Mail*, *Sunday Mirror*, David Williams, Sian Roderick, Hywel Davis, Mario Basini, and Wyn Holloway.

I am particularly indebted to the following for their special contributions, guidance and support: Dewi Bowen for the drawings of the 'Roman Fort', 'John Charles', 'Disappearing Landmarks' and the plan of the Roman Fort; Lyon of the *Birmingham Gazette* for the Bryn Jones cartoon; John Lloyd, formerly of the *Daily Express*; John Rees, formerly editor of the *Western Mail*; Ken Jones, chief sports reporter of the *Independent*; Ray Parker, formerly of the *South Wales Echo*; John Hughes, formerly of the *Merthyr Express*; Neil Fowler, editor of the *Western Mail*; Geoffrey Rich, formerly editor of the *South Wales Echo*; Phil Shaw, of the *Independent*; Judith and Geraint Roberts; Ann and Jason Watkins; grandchildren Jenny and Matthew Roberts; Chris Riordan, Ray Tucker, Carolyn Jacobs, Anthony Hughes, Rhian Pratt, as well as James Howarth and all the editorial staff at Tempus Publishing.

Whilst I have made every effort to trace copyright on this collection, to discover the provenance of every item has proved impossible. If I have inadvertently used material in breach of copyright and without proper acknowledgement then I do apologise.